CW00432657

Your Garden Year

by
Jean Miller

Published in the UK by
POWERFRESH Limited
21 Rothersthorpe Crescent
Northampton
NN4 8JD

Telephone   0845 130 4565
Facsimile   0845 130 4563
E Mail   info@powerfresh.co.uk

Copyright © 2004
Cover and interior layout by Powerfresh
Illustrations Sanjit Saha

ISBN   1904967043

Printed in Belgium by
Proost N.V. International Book Production
Powerfresh September 2004

"The best book on gardening for all of us is the book of our own practical experience."

Joseph Jacob

This is sound advice since, depending in which part of the country you garden, the weather will create a give/take precedence to your tasks. So it is better to create your own notes of do's and don't's to suit the contents of your garden.

Use the personal note pages to remind yourself of the what and when of monthly tasks or, what I think of, as pleasures. After all, you are in your garden and should be savouring most aspects of it.

Spring

Spring and the sap is rising and so can the gardener's blood pressure. Panic sets in and a vision of the whole season of garden tasks parades before you.

That is the whole point. You don't have to do it all at once. Start now and gently pace the work. It's all starting to happen anyway, so go with the flow.

"For, lo, the winter is past, the rain is over and gone."

Song of Solomon

March

This will be a stop/start month. The weather could still be wintry but there will be days to wander around the garden admiring the spring bulbs, the birds returning to nest and the sheer joy of having a garden.

The sting in the tail of all this communing with nature is that, miss out now on seasonal jobs, you will be rushing to catch up for some time to come.

Start now!

"Whatever I have to do has not yet begun. It is March."

William Stanley Mervin

March Reminders

Paths

Make sure garden paths are negotiable. You need to use them safely to access beds. Watch out for algae and moss.

Borders

Clear away any remaining leaves to show emerging stems against the damp black soil. This will be the only time to have such a fresh sparkling look. It can give a sense of husbandry, or smugness, whichever way you want to take it. It doesn't last!

Sheds and Outbuildings

Check all outbuildings for signs of dampness. Fences and walkways may need repairing. You will not want to be bogged down with any of this later on — the plants will be calling you.

Pruning

Most shrubs need pruning after a spring flowering. Prune trees to keep them in shape - better before the sap starts rising. Hybrid tea roses should be pruned hard back to a goblet shape.

Flowers

Plant summer-flowering bulbs.
Sow hardy annuals outside in borders.
Divide any compacted clumps of perennials.

Lawns

If dry enough, give the lawns a first cut with
the mower blades set high. Repair lawn
edges. Apply fertiliser.

Greenhouse

Make sure all is shipshape to start the
sowing of bedding and salad plants.

Ponds

Check there are enough oxygenating plants.
Divide marginal plants. Start feeding the
fish.

March - Notes

Jot down extra jobs that your particular garden needs and have the satisfaction of ticking them off this list. This applies to all the note pages.

March - Notes

March - Notes

March - Notes

March - Notes

April

April is known as the unpredictable month. With good reason. Sunshine, showers and even snow will all be possible to try the gardener.

Spirits will rise with the temperature. A feeling of expectancy in the air bourne out by shoots and buds showing all over the place, making the garden a source of new interests.

Higher temperatures with lengthening days will be an added bonus. There may even be time to "stand and stare".

"I have seen the Lady April bringing the daffodils.
Bringing the Spring grass and the soft warm April rain."

John Masefield

April Reminders

Flowers and Borders

Continue to clean up beds and borders. Finish dividing large clumps of perennials to make way for new planting. Start staking. It may look ungainly but saves trouble in borders later. Deadhead bulb flowers such as narcissi as they fade. Feed around base of plant but leave the leaves until they die off.

Lawns

Grass can be cut more often now. Watch out for and lift out with a weed - fork any weeds as they appear. Raking and scarifying will remove moss and thatch.

Trees and Shrubs

These will benefit from mulching to conserve moisture, making sure that the ground is already well watered.

Ponds

Fish should be taking up feed now. Blanket weed could be forming but is easily lifted out with a cane.

April - Notes

This is the time to list any bulbs you have seen in other gardens, ready to add to your planting in Autumn.

April - Notes

April - Notes

April - Notes

April - Notes

April - Notes

May

The merry month of May will not be so if you haven't kept up from the begining!

The weather should be settling down and the garden will be full of blossom for the bees and other pollinating insects.

You will now think that this is what it's all about. A lovely summer garden is starting to happen because of you.

'Loveliest of trees, the cherry now Is hung with bloom along the bough."

A E Housman

May Reminders

Containers and Hanging Baskets

These can be planted up now but don't put them in their final positions outdoors until all risk of frost has gone.

Borders

There is still time to sow hardy annuals early in the month.

Keep on top of deadheading.

Lawns

Grass can be cut regularly now, lowering the mower blades to suit the type of lawn you want. Neaten the edging of the lawn to give a crisp finish. This really does make it better.

Shrubs

Prune back forsythia stems that have already flowered.

Ponds

These need to be checked for returning blanket weed. Water plants can be lifted and divided.

May - Notes

The names of interesting plants will not be remembered if
you don't get them down in your little book - this one!

May - Notes

May - Notes

May - Notes

Summer time. The hazy lazy days of summer should be yours. The pottering season has begun.

Use your garden as intended. Lazy lunches. Barbeques and Sundowners and, of course, swapping plants with friends. Enjoy it all.

"Summer afternoon - summer afternoon; to me those have always been the two most beautiful words in the English language."

Henry James

June

The month of the longest day.

Twilight in the garden is a magical time. To stroll around when all is still and scents waft on the air is one one of the greatest pleasures.

'*O suns and skies and clouds of June,*
And flowers of June together,
Ye cannot rival for one hour."

Helen Hunt Jackson

June Reminders

Plants and Borders

Regular deadheading and watering is the key to a fresh looking garden. Check that plants are staked well and wall plants tied in.

Containers

Tender plants in pots can go outdoors now to decorate paths and terraces or to provide visual points of interest.

Hedges

Depending on growth rates hedges will need clipping to maintain good shapes.

Consider some simple topiary. Children will love it.

Pools

Ensure that small children cannot tumble into pools.

June - Notes

In a more relaxing mood, you will be making plans or alterations. Get them down now, however vague, before they waft away on the summer air.

June - Notes

June - Notes

June - Notes

June - Notes

June - Notes

July

This is high summer.

Gentle days. Just keeping the garden ticking over. Or, perhaps, trips away to other gardens.

"April is in my mistress' face
And July in her eyes hath place.'

Thomas Morley

July Reminders

Plants and Borders

Deadheading can be a pleasant job in early morning giving an opportunity to be aware of what's going on.
Herbs need clipping into shape or cutting back after flowering.

Lawns

Lawns can still be fed and aerated. Water if dry.

Ponds

Water levels in ponds need constant checking. Keep cleaning pump filters as fish need running water.

Containers

Lillies can be transferred from the pots they have been grown in and placed in gaps in borders for instant effect.

Watering

When watering with a hosepipe, consider the vulnerable spots as the hose is dragged around bed edges. Strategic posts or stops can prevent plant damage.

July - Notes

The ideas gleaned from other gardens should be listed. For example, new plants and possible colour schemes.

July - Notes

July - Notes

July - Notes

August

The last month of Summer. Treat yourself by having days off.

Sunny days demand cool drinks in the shade. Pile up the cushions, put your feet up and read or just doze.

Don't think about weeds. Tell yourself there aren't any!

'Untroubling and untroubled where I lie —
The grass below — above the vaulted sky."

John Clare

August Reminders

Take time to sit down at various points in the garden to consider how well certain areas or borders have done. Now is the time to consider a better scheme. Jot it down in your notes now! You will forget.

Shrubs and Hedges

This is the last month for real cutting and clipping of shrubs and hedges in case of frosts taking off new growth.

Plants and Borders

Lavenders need trimming right back to maintain a real shape, avoiding the old established wood.

Keep deadheading new growth and tie in unruly climbers.

Lawns

Lawn growth will be slowing down. Heighten blades on the mower.

August - Notes

Remind yourself of garden centre visits and nurseries to hunt down special plants. Supplies will be running out now. List any failures and any replacements.

August - Notes

August - Notes

August - Notes

Autumn

Seasons of mists and general thankfulness that there isn't much to do now.

Enjoy choosing new bulb displays and start planting according to the relevant month.

*"O Wild West Wind,
thou breath of Autumn's being."*

Percy Bysshe Shelley

September

This month could turn into an Indian summer. Autumn has barely come but come it will — make the most of golden days.

"The days grow short when you reach September."

Helen Hunt Jackson

September Reminders

Lawns

Seed any bare patches in lawns and water during dry spells.

Ponds

Fish may not take as much food now. Untouched food will just foul the water.

Plants and Borders

Bulbs are coming into garden centres. Plant as soon as you can according to requirements. This can be frustrating if the weather turns nasty. Little and often is the trick.

Check that any climbers have not gone into guttering. Turn your back and off they go.

Border plants if still well staked will extend the wellbeing of the garden and you!

There is still time to enjoy the garden.

September- Notes

List bulbs to buy. Decide on titles for winter reading and stock up. Or drop hints.

September- Notes

September- Notes

September- Notes

September- Notes

September- Notes

October

Bright days will keep you going out but crisp ones will send you indoors.
Work done now will save panic time in the Spring.

"October's bright blue weather."

Helen Hunt Jackson

October Reminders

Plants and Borders

Don't be too tidy in the borders as old flower stems will protect new shoots from frost.

Little and often also applies to fallen leaves, protecting lawns and making the job easier, watch your leaf mould grow into next year's mulch.

Containers

Plants in pots should be moved to a more sheltered spot, if not to a greenhouse.
This will have to be ready to receive overwintering plants.

Ponds

A pond will need netting over since a sudden leaf drop could ruin the pond balance. Remeber to leave spaces in the netting for the passage of wild life.

October- Notes

Take stock of any necessary alterations and list new ideas.

October- Notes

October- Notes

October- Notes

Shorter days and colder nights with possible frosts and even an odd snow shower does not make this the most popular month for the gardener.

'November's sky is chill and drear,
November's leaf is red and sear."

Sir Walter Scott

November Reminders

Containers

Protect large pots that cannot be moved. Bubble-wrap will protect if not enhance.

Ponds

Fish will not need feeding and frogs will settle in nooks and crannies for the winter.

Catching Up

A pleasant time can be had in heated greenhouses and sheds, cleaning tools and pulling out the mower to be serviced.

Make sure that bird feeding stations are in place and that access to them is safe for you in poor weather. In very bad weather don't do it. The birds won't thank you for breaking a hip.

November - Notes

A good time for making up shopping lists. For example for twine, canes, and compost but also for bulbs, roses, shrubs and trees to kick-start next season.

November - Notes

November - Notes

November - Notes

Winter

The season for fireside dreaming and dozing,

"If Winter comes,
can Spring be far behind?"

Percy Bysshe Shelley

December

The dark days before Christmas.

Garden centres are much more appealing than forays into the garden. A cold gardener is not a happy one.

'We are nearer to Spring
Than we were in September.
I heard a bird sing
In the dark of December."

Oliver Herford

December Reminders

Do whatever you can. The days are too short and it really is gardeners' tea and toast time with catalogues and thinking how you can use the branches and berries for festive decorations.

You've earned your rest.

December- Notes

A good time to list possible presents for fellow gardeners.
And yourself!

December- Notes

December- Notes

December- Notes

December- Notes

December- Notes

January

The year has turned! There is now hope and the excitement of starting afresh.

Enthusiasm is no substitute for common sense. Don't work in the cold.

"January grey is here."

Percy Bysshe Shelley

January Reminders

Depending on location, and there is no greater climate change from north to south than at this time — almost Spring in the favoured southwest, not so in the northeast — you will have to decide what is possible in *your* garden.

If a burst of sunshine, or energy, finds you in the garden, do check on possible ice in the pond. Hot water poured on gently will melt any ice without causing the shock wave that a hard thump with a stick would produce, possibly killing the fish.

January - Notes

List your Great Improvements. You may even get them done.

January- Notes

January- Notes

January- Notes

February

The thin sharp light of this month will pull you into the garden.

Discovering buds and emerging shoots, which will be there, is deeply satisfying.

'If you ask me why I love best
this month of all the year,
It is because my garden breathes
that Spring is in the air."

Quoted by S Graveson in My Villa Garden, 1915.

February Reminders

Beds and Borders

Snowdrops can be divided 'in the green'. To split up in this way will help to increase your stock. Who can have too many snowdrops?

Pruning

Towards the end of the month, start cutting back late-flowering clematis.

Depending on weather, hard prune buddleia. Wisteria now needs its winter prune, finishing the July pruning - if you did!

Take a deep breath, it's all about to happen and it's going to be lovely.

February - Notes

Now is the time to note the best effects viewed from the house windows in the winter months.

February - Notes

February - Notes

February - Notes

In short

*"There is no season such delight
can bring,
As Summer, Autumn, Winter, and
the Spring. "*

Wiliam Browne, 1591 -1643